Axolotls
for Beginners

Species Appropriate Care for the Mexican Water Monsters

D1636846

ALINA DARIA

Contents

What are axolotls?

Axolotls (*Ambystoma mexicanum*) are caudata amphibians but are often mistakenly thought to be reptiles. They are classified in the family of the mole salamanders (*genus Ambystoma*). Both size and expected lifespan can vary greatly in some cases. As a rule, axolotls grow to between 15 and 30 centimetres (*between 6 and 12 inches*) and weigh between 50 and 300 grams (*between 2 and 10 ounces*). However, there are also specimens that grow up to 40 centimetres (*16 inches*).

Most axolotls live between ten and twenty years. Occasionally, however, some axolotls have been known to live up to 25 years. Axolotls need cool and oxygen-rich water. They are not solitary animals and should therefore be kept at least in pairs. Many owners decide to keep three animals. These should be about the same size!

Axolotls have external gills, and their lungs are not fully developed. Although they can switch between land and water for short periods, they should spend their lives in water as they are not adult moles but remain in the larval stage. The colder it is, the more often axolotls voluntarily go ashore.

The name *axolotl* comes from Aztec, or more precisely from the Aztec language *Náhuatl*. It is a compound word made up of *Atl* and *Xolotl*.

Atl means *water* and *Xolotl* stands for *monster* but is also the name of an Aztec god. Axolotls probably got the name *water monster* because of their appearance, although nowadays many people find the little amphibians very cute and not monster-like.

Axolotls have their home in Mexico and are not too common in the wild. They lived in Lake Chalco, Lake Xochimilco and a few other bodies of water in Mexico. These are mainly stagnant waters and lakes.

The lakes mentioned are located in a volcanic basin near Mexico City. Today, they are largely dry, and the water bodies are only sparsely developed.

Another problem is the heavy water pollution in the axolotl's native habitat. For these reasons, the animal is threatened with extinction and will probably not be found in the wild for too much longer. Axolotls are now far more common among hobbyists and breeders and are therefore highly domesticated.

© KinEnriquez

In 1805, Alexander von Humboldt, a German explorer, returned from an expedition in Mexico and brought back two axolotls. He wanted to study them more closely. Many years later, in 1863, a French research team brought a somewhat larger group of axolotls from Mexico to France. Over the years, the little animals were studied more and more intensively before they established themselves much later as popular pets.

The heads of axolotls are rounded and large, their limbs are relatively short. The eyes are wide apart. Behind the eyes they each have three gill branches that can be actively moved. Their tail is flat, has fin seams and is very long. Axolotls use their tail to control their swimming direction. Usually, the males have a slightly longer tail than the females.

What is special about axolotls is that although they grow steadily and also become reproductively mature, they always remain larvae. This peculiarity of axolotls is due to their limited thyroid function - hormones are produced in the thyroid gland of a living creature that are responsible, among other things, for the development of a larvae into an adult. Axolotls, however, have a malfunctioning thyroid gland, which is why they never become a 'proper' adult amphibian. Metamorphosis is therefore not possible for them. Through the external addition of artificial hormones, an axolotl can indeed develop into an adult caudate and then have a similar appearance to a tiger salamander, but this should be avoided. While an axolotl can live for ten to twenty years as a larva, it can only live for about five years if artificial hormones are administered. Life expectancy is therefore drastically shortened.

The permanent state in the larval stage is called neoteny. Although axolotls always remain larvae, they can of course reproduce.

Axolotls can regenerate their bodies very well and usually completely, as they are able to regrow their limbs, organs and even brain parts. How this is possible is still not fully understood. Research into the regenerative properties of axolotls is still ongoing. It is hoped that the research results and findings can also be applied in human medicine. However, some things have already been discovered. Axolotls have connective tissue cells that virtually reverse their development.

The special body cells *fibroblasts* develop again into precursor cells that can form bones as well as skin and tendons. Thus, the regeneration of different types of connective tissue is possible. However, the adaptation to humans is proving difficult in research - humans also have fibroblasts. In the case of an injury, however, the human fibroblasts do not develop back into precursor cells, but they continue to develop into myofibroblasts - and these form the scar tissue in humans.

The genome of an axolotl is extremely complex. It is ten times as large as the genome of a human, as it has over thirty billion base pairs. Therefore, decoding this genome is not easy. However, it has already been researched that axolotls have some genes that are only found in them and other amphibian species. These genes are active in regenerating tissue.

The axolotl's natural reproductive season is in spring. Female axolotls usually produce between 80 and 700 eggs, which they lay on aquatic plants. These eggs are not always actually fertilised. If fertilised, axolotls hatch after about 10 to 20 days. Males reach reproductive maturity at about one to two years of age. Females usually become reproductively mature earlier and can reproduce after about one year.

© KinEnriquez

© KinEnriquez

Types and colours

Since this is a book for beginners, we will not go into the exact breeding forms and combinations, but only look at the superficial subdivision of the different types. The axolotl types can be roughly divided into four categories:

1. Albinos

2. Coppers

3. Whites (Leucistic)

4. Wildlings (Melanoid)

Albinos are white or yellowish and can also be somewhat shiny or shimmery. Their eggs are white. Due to an enzyme defect, albinos do not have melanin, which would otherwise cause a darker colouration. The enzyme that albinos do not have is tyrosinase (amino acid = tyrosine).

Coppers come in many colours, such as yellow, brown, white, copper. They can also shimmer a little. Their eggs are beige/light brown. In contrast to the albinos, they do have tyrosine or tyrosinase, but they do not produce melanin either, only phaeomelanin. Phaeomelanin is a pigment which, together with eumelanin (also a pigment), determines the colour of the skin.

In whites (leucistics), the pigment cells are not formed. This is called leucism. The melanin, which causes a dark colouration, does not leave the neural crest and is therefore not found on the skin. If this were to happen, it would not be leucistic but wild/melanoid. Their eggs are dark. By the way: Albinos are different though - albinos develop all pigment cells normally, but albinos generally lack melanin.

Wildlings (melanonids) are usually black and/or brown. Sometimes a yellowish colouration occurs. Their eggs are also dark.

The colour of the eggs does not (always) indicate what the larva will look like later. The colour of the eggs depends on the colour of the mother. However, the colouration of the emerging larva does not depend on the mother alone, but on both parents.

Unfortunately, in some countries axolotls have been dyed or given colour pigments so that they "shine" in numerous bright colours (red, pink, green etc.). It is not advisable to buy a dyed animal.

© *Tinwe*

Males and females

Male axolotls usually have a slightly longer tail than females. Males also always have a swollen cloacal region, even outside the breeding season. This is not the case with females. However, the gender can only be determined after about one year, or when they are about twenty centimetres big.

A male reaches reproductive maturity at about one to two years. Females usually become reproductively mature earlier and can reproduce after about one year.

As in many other species, the male performs a "mating dance" at breeding time to "seduce" the female. During the mating dance, the male has his long tail towered, wags it back and forth and also nudges the female to encourage her to mate.

The females usually produce around 80 to 700 eggs and lay them on water plants. This happens about every two months. The eggs are not always actually fertilised. When fertilised, a small axolotl develops inside the egg - this process is called *paedogenesis*. Usually, axolotls hatch after about 10 to 20 days. They then feed on the yolk for a few more days.

The babies are already born independently and can move around without any problems. After five weeks they measure about five to six centimetres.

As axolotls are not solitary animals, they should be kept at least in pairs.

Of course, if you have only males, egg-laying will never occur. Some owners prefer this.

The eggs - or the hatched larvae - are often eaten. Some keepers also remove the eggs and freeze them first, as they die from freezing. Under no circumstances should they be disposed of directly but must be frozen beforehand if removed! From a moral point of view, some people have a problem with this. This is understandable. If you do not want to release the eggs/larvae for eating and you also don't want to freeze the eggs, it is best to keep only male axolotls.

Axolotls living together should be about the same size so that the larger axolotl does not - voluntarily or involuntarily - attack or try to swallow the smaller axolotl. Smaller axolotls are easily eaten by larger ones. As a worst-case scenario, the smaller axolotl may be even too big to eat and may get stuck in the mouth of the larger axolotl. Both animals can die from this! It is therefore very important that the animals are approximately the same size.

Behaviour

Axolotls have their home in stagnant waters and lakes near Mexico City, so they do not like water flows. They usually stay close to the bottom or directly on the bottom. In a home tank, too, it can usually be observed that axolotls feel most comfortable at the bottom.

Axolotls like to hide and can become stressed if they have no hiding places. Hiding places for them are not only shelters, caves, tubes, etc., but also simple cold-water plants. However, the accessories should not have any sharp edges, as axolotls can easily injure themselves on them.

Ideally, the water plants should not be placed directly at the edge of the tank but should be at least ten centimetres away from the edge. Axolotls use the lateral line system for orientation and therefore like to move along the tank walls.

As axolotls are nocturnal, many of the animals like to stay somewhat hidden during the day and only come out in the evening.

It is therefore good for the plants if a suitable lamp is also purchased for the tank. The lamp promotes good growth of the aquatic plants and prevents too many algae from settling in the tank. The light of the lamp should be white, not blue.

© *alejandrohcruz*

Getting the axolotls

When buying a pet, many people first turn to the traditional and established pet shop. Unfortunately, however, pet shops often give the wrong advice. This is not only the case with axolotls, but also with other popular pets such as rabbits, hamsters, etc. Therefore, the information you get in the pet shop should be taken with a pinch of salt.

Also, pet shops often sell axolotls that should not be given away. Some animals are injured or sick and are sold anyway. Also, you often don't get an up-to-date BD test (please see 'Common Diseases') in the pet shop and can therefore easily catch pathogens.

In addition, pet shops often sell axolotls that are too small and not yet ready to be given away. Axolotls should be at least ten centimetres big when they are handed over. In most cases, this size is reached at the age of three to four months.

It is therefore a better alternative to buy axolotls from a reputable breeder or to take them second-hand. The animals should naturally look healthy and have no injuries. Also, an up-to-date BD test should be presented at the time of delivery to ensure that you do not bring this fatal disease into your home - more on BD in the chapter "Common Diseases".

A reputable breeder will prepare the animals ready for transport. It is best to take a food-safe box with you to pick up the animals, which can later be used as a quarantine box. The breeder will pack the axolotl(s) in a suitable transport bag. The bag should be about one third full of cold water and two thirds air. These bags should be carefully placed in the transport box. The exact procedure should be discussed before collection.

If the axolotl is to be transported in summer, it is best to take cool packs or a large cool box with you. This ensures that the water does not heat up (too much) during transport.

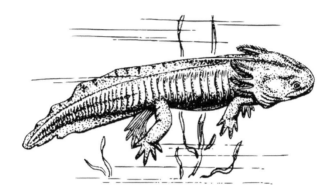

© OpenClipart-Vectors

The home

Axolotls are relatively easy to care for and feel comfortable in a species-appropriate tank. Two to three axolotls should have at least 0.5 square metres (*5 square feet*) of space available. For example, a 200-litre tank measuring 100 cm x 50 cm x 40 cm (*roughly 40 inches x 20 inches x 15 inches*) is great. The height of the tank is not too relevant; more important is the floor space of at least half a square metre (*at least five square feet*). Of course, the home may also be larger; the more space, the better!

The axolotl's home should be angular - a rounded shape should be avoided, otherwise the animals will not be able to orientate themselves well. It should also be made of glass; plastic is rather unsuitable. The tank does not need a cover. It is even better if the tank is open, as these do not heat up as much as closed tanks. An open tank is also easier to handle when cleaning and feeding. If cats or similar are also kept at the same time, the tank can also be protected with a sturdy grid lid so that other animals are kept away from the axolotls.

Most axolotl keepers agree that the water temperature is probably the most important criterion for good keeping. As already mentioned, axolotls need cool and oxygen-rich water. Clean, high-quality tap water is usually sufficient. Fertiliser and starter bacteria are not necessary. Water conditioners can also be dispensed with.

The optimal water temperature is between about 10°C and 20°C (*between 50°F and 68°F*). In case of emergency, the temperature can be up to a maximum of 22°C (*72°F*), but this should be a major exception. If the water temperature is too high, axolotls feel extremely stressed and are more susceptible to diseases.

Especially in the summer months, the temperature can become a problem. If the temperature is too high, the risk of fungal disease is also greatly increased. However, if the temperature drops too much and is less than 10°C (*less than 50°F*), the metabolism of the axolotl is slowed down, and this can be very hard on the digestion.

It is optimal if domesticated axolotls also sense different temperatures in the different seasons. This helps them to better assess the season and the reproductive periods - because ideally no eggs should be spawned from summer to autumn. In winter, for example, axolotls can be kept at a water temperature of 12°C (*53°F*) and this can be increased to 16°C (*61°F*) in summer.

In most countries it is therefore unavoidable to use a cooling fan or a cooling unit.

Cooling fans have the effect of lowering the prevailing temperature in relation to the room air temperature. They can usually lower the air by up to

5°C; of course, it always depends on the particular device. In countries where it is very hot in summer, a cooling fan will not be sufficient. For example, if the room temperature is 30°C (*85°F*), even a cooling fan will not be able to keep the axolotl at a temperature suitable for its species.

For many people, a cooling unit is the better alternative. These keep the temperature constantly cool, even if the owner is not at home for a few days. The purchase costs are usually quite high, but the purchase pays off in almost all cases. If axolotls are to live in countries that get quite warm or even hot in summer, such cooling is absolutely necessary - anything else would not be appropriate for the animal and another pet might be more suitable.

It is also a good idea to place the tank in a room that is relatively cool, even in summer, or at least not exposed to direct sunlight. Of course, the axolotl's home can also be in the cellar.

When the tank is filled with water for the first time, bacteria should settle in the water filter as well as on the bottom. These are important for the metabolic cycle and are not harmful. The accumulating "rubbish" - i.e., the droppings of the axolotl and the dead plant remains - are first converted into ammonium, ammonia and then into nitrite and nitrate. How long the conversion of nitrite into nitrate takes depends on various factors; for example, on how many (real!) plants there are in the tank. At best, the plants should be robust.

10 water plants that are well suited to the axolotl tank:

1. Waterweed

2. Java Fern / Java Moss

3. Moss

4. Spathiphyllum

5. Anubias

6. Fanwort

7. Hornwort

8. Mouse-Ear Chickweed

9. Horseradish / Water Radish

10. Sword plants (Echinodorus)

Excessive hygiene can do more harm than good. Although excess nitrate and other germs should be removed during cleaning, the bottom and the filter should not be cleaned too meticulously. More on this later!

The filter should ideally be an external filter that is suitable for the size of the tank. Plastic internal filters are less suitable. The pipe should be just below the water surface so that the surface moves, but the axolotls don't notice too much - they don't like currents, preferring still or stagnant water. Starter bacteria are not necessary. The important bacteria form during the cycling phase and a balance is achieved in the tank in a natural way. However, a bottom filter is also possible.

Furthermore, it is advisable to place the tank on a stable surface. It should be easy for people to reach so that cleaning and changing the water can be done comfortably. The piece of furniture on which the tank is to stand should be able to withstand a load of at least 200 kilograms (*at least 440 pounds*).

Axolotls should have some hiding places available. These should of course be disinfected beforehand - as should the entire accessories - so that no pathogens are introduced into the home. Axolotls also use plants to hide behind, but some caves etc. should be available.

At least one hiding place should be provided per axolotl so that the axolotls do not fight over the hiding places. Wood is not suitable. Coconut caves are popular because of their appearance, but they are not suitable either. The accessories should be made of stone or clay.

It is a good idea to bake this in the oven before use to kill pathogens. Ideally, ovenproof accessories should be baked in the oven at 200°C (*approx. 390°F*) for about one to two hours. Tubes and caves are usually particularly popular.

Waterweed © Couleur

Water

If you live in a region with high-quality tap water, this is perfectly fine as tank water. The quality of tap water varies from country to country - and there are also sometimes big regional differences.

If in doubt, the water can first be tested for chlorine, heavy metals and the like. Chlorine is extremely harmful to axolotls and other aquatic life.

The water hardness should be about 15 °e/°Clark to 25 °e/°Clark (*210 ppm/°aH to 350 ppm/°aH*). It should not fall below 10 °e/°Clark (*140 ppm/°aH*).

The carbonate hardness (alkalinity) should be above 6 °e/°Clark (*90 ppm/°aH*). It is ideal between 6 °e/°Clark and 12 °e/°Clark (*90 ppm/°aH and 180 ppm/°aH*).

The pH-value should be between 7 and 8; a pH-value of 6.5 to 6.9 is also OK. In general, most breeders recommend a pH-value between 7.0 and 7.5.

Other very important factors are nitrite, nitrate and ammonia. Ammonia or ammonium is formed in the tank water by food residues, dead plant parts etc. Then nitrite is formed from this, which in turn forms nitrate. How long the transformation takes often varies and depends on the conditions and the equipment of the tank.

The ammonia level (NH3) should be less than 0.2 mg per litre *(0.2 ppm)*.

The nitrate level (NO3) should be a maximum of 25 mg per litre *(25 ppm)*. Above a value of 40 mg per litre *(40 ppm)* it becomes toxic!

The nitrite level (NO2) should always be zero. A very low value is OK at times but should never exceed

0.5 mg per litre (*0.5 ppm*) (toxic!). If the value does rise above this, the animals should first be moved into food-safe plastic boxes with cold water until the value has been lowered again.

Some axolotls occasionally try to jump out of the tank. If you have an open tank, the gap between the water surface and the edge of the tank should be at least ten centimetres (*at least four inches*) so that the animals cannot jump out. Otherwise, of course, a cover made of solid wire can help.

The water level should be at least twenty to thirty centimetres (*at least eight to twelve inches*). It also depends on how large the tank is overall. Each axolotl should have at least 60 to 100 litres of water available (*at least 16 to 26 gallons per axolotl*). The more water there is in the tank, the better the biological and bacterial balance. It is therefore better to let in too much water than too little. Nevertheless, it is advisable - regardless of whether there is a cover or not - to leave an air space of about ten centimetres (*four inches*), as the axolotls like to swim to the surface and stick their little heads out of the water.

Once you have cleaned the tank, washed the substrate and added the tank water, the tank is not yet ready for the axolotl. First of all, there is what is known as a cycling phase.

After about one day, the cold-water plants can be added. After that, however, the values have to settle down before the axolotls can move in. This cycling phase can last up to eight weeks. It always depends on the water values, which should be tested regularly until a healthy and species-appropriate bacterial fauna has been established. When the water values have settled in the range described above, the animals can move into their new home.

During this phase, it may happen that the plants weaken somewhat or even die off partially, as the nutrient balance in the tank is not yet optimal. This is not a problem. If necessary, the plants can be replaced or supplemented after the cycling phase has been completed.

Opinions are also divided on the duration of the cycling phase. Some breeders say four weeks is enough, others recommend at least six to eight weeks. In case of doubt, it is of course better to let the phase run too long than too short, to be sure that the water quality is good enough and the balance has settled down. The water filter must also already be in operation during this phase. The plants should already have moved into the new home, as they are essential for the water values and the balance to be achieved. During this phase it is not necessary to change the water.

It is advisable to test the water values regularly from the second week onwards. The nitrite value will rise sharply and reach a so-called peak. As explained before, the nitrite value should always be around zero. In the cycling phase, however, it can rise sharply and even reach a value of 1. This is then the peak. When the nitrite value has reached zero again, the axolotls can move into their new home. If you want to speed up the reduction of the nitrite value, you can add very small amounts of food or axolotl faeces to the tank water.

When the nitrite peak occurs is difficult to predict and very dependent on the individual conditions in the tank. In most cases, however, the peak occurs between the second and the sixth week of the cycling phase. It usually lasts about a week.

Once the axolotls have moved into their new home, a water change is carried out regularly, although not all the water is changed. It is recommended to change about 30 to 40 percent of the water. How often this is done depends on how good or bad the water values are. Most owners and breeders perform a water change every two, three or four weeks.

© *Tinwe*

Bottom of the tank

The bottom of the tank is a very common topic of contention in the axolotl community. Unfortunately, it often happens that axolotls swallow the small or large stones on the bottom, as they are "suction snappers". Whether this is harmful depends on the size and the number of objects swallowed. Blockages can occur, sometimes unfortunately fatal.

In Germany, light-coloured pebbles are recommended as substrate. The pebbles should not be artificially coloured. Black gravel and/or gravel coated with plastic should be avoided in particular, as this is toxic to the axolotl if swallowed and can also poison the water.

In addition, many black stones also give off iron. A size of one millimetre to three millimetres is the standard in Germany. The edges should not be sharp but rounded. Larger stones can lead to blockages and often cannot be excreted.

However, in English speaking countries such as the US, it is not recommended to use pebbles. It is correct that on occasions the axolotls swallow the little stones. If they are small enough, the axolotls usually defecate them. However, there is indeed a risk of constipation.

A good alternative is the use of sand as a substrate. Swallowing sand is usually considered harmless because sand is very small and fine. However, sand swirls up quite easily and can make the water look a bit cloudy. It also requires good maintenance and needs to be dug up regularly. The reason for this is that rotting may occur in the sand, for example.

There are a lot of axolotl owners who do not use substrate at all, especially in the US. This can be problematic as the axolotl would have a better grip when walking if there is substrate. Also, a film of bacteria can form on the bare bottom and the stability / natural balance in the tank may be impaired.

If you use substrate, it should be rinsed off before use, for example under the shower with the help of a sieve. The tank water may otherwise become cloudy if the substrate has not been cleaned. The bottom can then be covered before the tank water is let in. When letting in the water, make sure that the substrate is not swirled up (too much), but remains nice and even.

Cleaning the tank

It is recommended to do a rough cleaning of the tank about every two weeks. The major cleaning only needs to be done about every four months.

During the rough cleaning, the plants as well as the accessories are removed from the tank. The bottom is vacuumed, for example with a substrate cleaner (hose). The plants are washed under running water. Depending on the size of the respective plant, this can be done under a tap or in the shower. The objects are also washed under running water and ideally wiped down briefly. During the rough cleaning, the axolotls can remain in the tank; they do not necessarily have to be taken out. It is recommended to change about 30 to 40 percent of the water.

However, during the major cleaning every four months, the axolotls must be removed from the tank. They can wait during the cleaning in boxes that have been filled with cold water beforehand. The objects and plants are also removed from the tank. The filter is then switched off and removed.

It is important to note that excessive hygiene can be just as harmful as a lack of hygiene. Bacteria are not bad per se - in fact, they are very important for the metabolism and health of the animals. These bacteria mainly do not settle in the water itself, but rather at the bottom and at/in the filter.

Excess nitrate, which develops through the droppings of the axolotls and through dead plant parts, should be removed during cleaning - however, too meticulous cleaning of the bottom and the filter should be avoided, as one can run the risk of eliminating all "good" bacteria.

This is also one of the reasons why it is perfectly sufficient to clean the filter only during the major cleaning - i.e., about every four months. Filter cleaning two to three times a year is therefore ideal.

When the filter is cleaned, it is first emptied. It is sufficient to lightly squeeze out the sponges. The housing of the filter is cleaned and, if necessary, substrate is refilled. The hoses should also be cleaned briefly; then the filter can be reassembled and put into operation. The filter should not be out of operation for more than an hour - but cleaning usually does not take that long anyway.

Socialisation

Axolotls should only be kept with other axolotls and not mixed with other species. Keeping them together with other species can cause major problems. Beginners in particular should avoid socialisation altogether in order not to take any unnecessary risks.

Usually, axolotls are offered dead food - dead worms, small pieces of fish, pellets with a large proportion of animal protein and the like. However, some keepers also want to offer their axolotls living food. This is often not recommended, for good reasons.

The only creatures that can possibly be kept together with axolotls are endler's guppies, dwarf shrimps (*neocaridina*), bubble snails, post horn snails, cardinal fish and zebra danios. Please note, however, that these animals are eaten by the axolotls in 99% of cases!

All other animal species must never be kept together with axolotls! There are several reasons for this. Firstly, many animals are simply too big to eat, but this does not stop the axolotls from trying. There are often "accidents" where an axolotl tries to eat a large fish and it gets stuck in its mouth. This is not good for either the axolotl or the fish and can be fatal!

It is particularly bad when an axolotl tries to eat a catfish, for example. For one thing, a catfish is too big to be eaten anyway and will get stuck in its mouth. However, it also has barbs on the end of its head, which make removing the fish very dangerous! The barbs of the catfish hook into the mouth of the axolotl. Sometimes a skilled vet can cut it out, sometimes both animals die trying. This is just one example of many.

There are also fish species (even small ones which "look harmless") that nibble or suck on the axolotl. The gill branches or even the tail is particularly often injured in the process!

It is therefore safest and most advisable to keep axolotls only with other axolotls! Please do not confuse axolotls with Andersonis and do not keep them together either! Due to the similar appearance, the layman can sometimes confuse an axolotl with an Andersoni.

Andersoni only occur in the pattern/colours of the wild animal. With a size of 18 to 20 centimetres, Andersoni remain smaller than Axolotls. There is a risk that an adult axolotl will try to eat an Andersoni. In addition, Andersoni are diurnal, while Axolotls are nocturnal. Andersoni are still much more active than axolotls and often more aggressive.

Catfish - keeping together with axolotls is very dangerous!

© maxmann

Quarantine

Before an axolotl moves into its new home, it should first be kept in quarantine. The quarantine period is usually four to six weeks and is completed individually. Several axolotls should not be placed in the same quarantine box.

One food-safe plastic box per axolotl is used for quarantine. Of course, an axolotl can also be placed in another, empty tank if one is left. It is important that the quarantine home is square. Round boxes or other containers are not suitable, as an axolotl orients itself to the walls (the so-called *lateral line system*).

The boxes should be able to hold about 10 to 15 litres of water (*about 2.7 to 4 gallons*). The lid does not need any holes, as axolotls absorb their oxygen through the water. The colder the water (ideally 12°C to 17°C / 53°F to 63°F), the higher the oxygen content of the water.

The plastic box is filled with cold, good quality (tap) water. If the tap water is of poor quality, water must be obtained elsewhere. The water is changed every day - not only a certain percentage, but all of it. Therefore, another box is needed for changing. The respective quarantine box should not only be emptied daily, but also thoroughly wiped out to remove bacteria and germs.

Quarantine boxes are particularly important in the following cases:

1. A completely new tank is set up in which no axolotls live yet. This must first be brought into a healthy equilibrium (see 'cycling phase'). In the meantime, the axolotls can spend their quarantine phase in the boxes described above.

2. A new axolotl is to be integrated into the group. Example: Only one axolotl was previously kept in solitary confinement (not species-appropriate!) or a

new friend is to enrich the existing group. Regardless of whether this axolotl comes from a breeder or a previous owner: the quarantine period should be completed so that the new axolotl does not introduce any pathogens and can first recover from the stress before it moves into its new home.

3. A slight illness has been detected, for example a fungal infection or a slight bite, and the affected axolotl should first recover, receive a salt bath or similar. Fungal infections should not be confused with more serious diseases - see the chapter on 'Common Diseases'.

Please always use salt without iodine!

© andreas160578

Diet

Axolotls are nocturnal hunters who lie in wait. They usually remain in one place and wait there for their prey. They do not actively search for food but wait for it at a fixed point and are therefore often very patient.

Their food includes almost everything they can overpower, for example insects and their larvae, worms, small fish and their eggs and small crustaceans. This can also be offered to a domesticated axolotl relatively easily and without much effort.

Axolotls either catch their prey as it swims by or they pick up their food from the bottom.

Most axolotls do not need to be fed daily; the larger the animal gets, the less often it needs food. Therefore, it is usually no problem to go away for the weekend and leave the animals alone for a few days. However, in the case of a longer absence, holiday care should be organised.

Adult axolotls can even fast for about ten days without suffering any damage. However, with a longer fasting period, there is a risk that axolotls will turn on each other and, in a worst-case scenario, injure or mutilate each other.

The feeding rhythm can be very individual, so always keep a close eye on the animals. If an axolotl gains a lot of weight, the time between two feedings should be extended. Overfeeding the animals should be taken very seriously and can often even lead to death.

Domesticated axolotls often do not select according to their natural instinct but eat whatever the owner makes available to them. Obesity can lead to diseases of the gastrointestinal tract, fatty liver and other feeding-related diseases.

As a general rule of thumb ...

... with a body size of up to 12 centimetres (*up to 4.7 inches*), axolotls should be fed every day.

... with a body size of up to about 16 centimetres (*up to about 6.3 inches*), they can be fed every two days.

... with a body size of up to about 18 centimetres (*up to about 7 inches*), they can be fed every three days.

... with a body size of more than 18 centimetres (*more than 7 inches*), they can be fed once or twice a week - most owners feed their adult animals only once a week.

To reiterate: These are only guidelines. The animals should always be closely observed to determine whether a normal body weight is maintained or whether the animal may be slowly tending towards obesity (fatty liver and other organs!). Accordingly, the fasting period can be extended or shortened.

Axolotls are carnivores (meat eaters). They cannot digest plant food efficiently and are therefore dependent on animal food. This is also the case, for example, with the generally popular domestic cat. It is best to offer the axolotls fresh food: small pieces of fish, worms (e.g., earthworms such as giant red worms/Dendrobena), small snails, small crustaceans and the like. Long worms are best cut up once before feeding.

However, it is not recommended to collect worms and other animals outside. It is possible for animals from the wild to introduce pathogens into the tank!

It is important to note that food should not be offered that is too large. The food must fit well in the mouth and must not cause the axolotl to swallow or get stuck in its mouth. If in doubt, it is better to cut the food into smaller, bite-sized pieces before feeding it!

Some owners also use pellets. However, great attention must be paid to the composition of these pellets, as they sometimes differ a lot. There are pellets that contain only 20-30% fish. You should also pay attention to whether the pellets are composed of high-quality animal food or whether unhealthy additives have been used for cost-cutting reasons.

In addition, pellets are offered on the market which have a high vegetable content. As axolotls are strict carnivores, these should not be used. Axolotls cannot utilise these vegetable components anyway. Therefore, pellets should consist of at least 60% animal protein!

It is also possible to feed frozen fish from the supermarket. Of course, the frozen fish should not be seasoned. It should also not have any bones. If bones are present, they must be removed before feeding. Fish should not be fed in too large pieces - therefore it should be cut into bite-sized pieces beforehand. For example, the pieces of fish can be 1 cm x 3 cm (*for example 0.4 inches x 1.2 inches*). Ideally, each axolotl should be fed five to six pieces per feeding. If worms, small crustaceans, pellets or small snails are also fed, the quantities should be adjusted individually.

Suitable fish species include trout, pike, pikeperch, eel, sturgeon, carp or perch. If possible, however, freshwater fish should be preferred in order to avoid the administration of iodine.

The meat of mammals such as chicken should not be fed. On the one hand, this is unnatural, as axolotls do not feed on chicken or similar meat in nature. Secondly, this type of meat is more difficult for axolotls to digest. Seaweed is also not suitable, as it naturally contains a high proportion of iodine. Iodine could cause axolotls to go into metamorphosis, which must be prevented.

Food remains can be easily removed with the help of food tongs.

Common diseases

BD (chytridiomycosis)

Axolotls should be tested for BD (*Batrachochytrium dendrobatidis*) at least once a year. The disease, also called chytridiomycosis, is often undetectable for months, but is very damaging to the axolotl's immune system and makes them more susceptible to further diseases. BD is a fungal disease. The chytridiomycosis fungus originates from Africa and causes an outbreak of chytridiomycosis in the tank. A few decades ago, the fungus found its way to Europe. It is considered the most common and dangerous disease for domesticated amphibians!

This fungus is extremely aggressive and causes mass amphibian mortality all over the world. Therefore, this disease is to be taken very seriously. The fungus is often transmitted via plants and other objects in the tank, especially if they have been taken over second-hand. Therefore, all plants and objects should be disinfected before use. However, BD can also be transmitted by fish, snails and other animals that may be placed in the axolotl's home (not recommended). If the keeping conditions are also not optimal, the chytrid fungus has an even easier game; for this reason, too, adequate water values and sufficient hygiene should always be ensured.

Symptoms of BD are, for example, black discoloured areas on the body of the axolotl - often on the lips or toes, but also in the area of the cloaca, the belly and the tail. One problem, however, is that black spots can also result from reproductive maturity. Therefore, this is somewhat difficult to distinguish - especially for a layperson. The fungus also likes to stay in the mucous membranes of the axolotl. It uses the animal as a host to multiply on.

BD can also be asymptomatic, especially in the beginning, so prevention is important. BD not only weakens the immune system and makes the axolotl more susceptible to further diseases, but in the worst case it can lead to the death of the animal, even if no symptoms are visible.

Another symptom of BD can be slimy gill hairs. A change in the animal's behaviour can also be a sign of BD, for example if the animal does not feel like eating or seems apathetic.

In case of a suspected case, a BD test should be carried out immediately, but even for animals without suspicion, an annual test is recommended to be on the safe side. Visibly ill animals should of course be taken to the vet immediately!

However, the animal does not necessarily have to be taken to the vet for the test. In many countries it is possible to take a swab at home and then take it to the vet or send it to the laboratory.

In case of an infestation or a positive test result, the entire tank and all furnishings must be thoroughly cleaned and disinfected. The pathogens are not visible to the naked eye as they only measure about 5 μm. It is therefore important to disinfect every area very thoroughly, for example with high-percentage alcohol (at least seventy percent).

Such intensive cleaning naturally also has the effect of removing the valuable bacteria cultures from the tank. Unfortunately, this cannot be avoided. Therefore, the bacteria have to re-colonise after the cleaning, which takes some time. For this reason, the water values should be kept well under control.

If a new axolotl is brought from the breeder or taken over from another owner, they should ideally provide an up-to-date BD test.

Fungal infections

Fungal infections can be recognised relatively well by the fact that they cause white spots on the axolotl's body or even white "fungal tufts". These can often be treated relatively well with salt baths. However, it is important to note that the salt used must not contain iodine.

For treatment, the animal is placed in a separate box filled with salt water. Approximately one teaspoon of salt is used per ten litres of water (*approx. 2.5 gallons*). The animal should spend several hours or at best even a whole day in the box. With this method, the salt content of the water is therefore low and the treatment time relatively long.

Another possibility is to intensify the salt bath. With this method, one teaspoon of salt per 1 litre (*per 0.25 gallons*) is added to the water in the box; however, the treatment time should then only be ten minutes!

Ideally, the axolotl should be kept in quarantine for about a week afterwards, so that it can be observed further, and it can be determined whether the fungal infection disappears completely.

To remove the fungal bacteria in the tank, it is a good idea to use sea almond leaves. Two leaves of the sea/tropical almond tree (*Terminalia catappa*) are added to 100 litres (*approx. 26 gallons*) of tank water. These have an antibacterial effect and also promote skin regeneration. The leaves do not have to be removed, but slowly decompose themselves.

Axolotl pest

Axolotl pest is a serious disease that leads very quickly to a deterioration in health, is quite aggressive and can cause the death of the animal if not treated. Therefore, the disease should be treated as soon as possible (within 24 hours!) by a competent veterinarian. It should not be confused with a simple fungal infection!

Axolotl pest is an infectious disease caused by mycobacteria. It is a mixture of bacteria and fungi. The pathogens are found in the soil as well as in the water and on their hosts, where they feed on dead biomass.

This disease also enjoys poor husbandry conditions such as poor water quality. Most dramatic here is water contamination by chlorine, nitrogen compounds and heavy metals. They occur, for example, when food remains are not removed and these slowly decompose. Inadequate and too infrequent water changes also favour this.

Symptoms of axolotl pest are, for example, changes in the skin, refusal of food up to emaciation, frayed fin areas and general reddening or bleeding on the animal's body. The spread of the disease over the whole body is extremely rapid in most cases and very large wound areas often develop. Home remedies do not help here; the diseases must be fought with suitable medication, which the veterinarian will prescribe. Treatment should not be delayed, as the disease unfortunately spreads very quickly and will most likely lead to the death of the animal. Often a vet will also prescribe healing baths with gentamycin or amphotericin, but this will be carefully investigated and prescribed by the expert vet.

Even with this infection, the entire tank including glass, objects and plants must be thoroughly cleaned and disinfected (ethanol/alcohol 70%). Many keepers even replace the entire equipment to be on the safe side. As with fungal infections, sea almond leaves can be added to the pathogen-free tank as a preventive measure.

(Bite) Injuries

Due to the axolotl's special ability to regenerate, minor injuries are often not a big problem. Many injuries, even slight bite wounds, heal by themselves. However, it is important to examine and observe the injury.

Unfortunately, sometimes an injury becomes infected or a fungal infection develops on the injured area. In such cases, the animal should of course be presented to a competent veterinarian. In the worst case, the vet may have to amputate one of the limbs.

However, in order for the limb to grow back, it is important that the respective area is not sewn up. This is another reason why it is essential that the vet treating the animal is well acquainted with axolotls. After treatment, the animal should first be kept in quarantine until the wound has largely closed.

After an amputation, wound healing first begins, the wound closes. This is followed by blastema formation and then blastema cell proliferation. Once this process is complete, new limb tissue is formed until, in the best case, a regenerated limb has emerged. However, the older the animal, the more difficult regeneration can be. If the animal is already of advanced age, it is also possible that the limb will only regenerate in a mutilated way.

<u>Obesity</u>

Axolotls readily accept the food offered and, in most cases, do not regulate their food intake independently in the home tank. It is therefore the owner's responsibility to regulate the food intake and to ensure that the animals do not become too fat. Being overweight can cause fatty degeneration of the liver and other organs. At first it may seem strange that adult axolotls go through such long periods of fasting (more on this in the diet chapter); however, overfeeding can have serious consequences and should therefore be avoided. Liver fatty degeneration can also impair osmosis, for example, and the likelihood of kidney failure is greatly increased.

The older an axolotl is, the slower its metabolism usually becomes. It is therefore a good idea to constantly monitor the animals and to react to impending obesity at an early stage in order to meet the individual needs of the animals.

An injured axolotl.

© *uthlas*

Epilogue

Axolotls are very special animals. Preparing to keep axolotls in a species-appropriate way requires a lot of time, knowledge and also incurs some costs. However, once everything has been set up and optimised, the axolotls can move in and are relatively easy-care pets.

Since they don't need to be fed very often in adulthood and don't need to be entertained by their owner, the time required is rather less than for other pets. The costs are also kept within reasonable limits after the first larger purchases, as axolotls do not need too much food. Running costs are, of course, the cooling unit, the water filter and so on. It should also be borne in mind that animals can fall ill unexpectedly, even if they are kept in the best conditions, and veterinary treatment can sometimes be costly. Therefore, you should always have enough savings to be able to react immediately in case of illness and to replace defective equipment, etc.

Finally, dear reader: For independent authors, product reviews are the basis for the success of a book. Therefore, we depend on your reviews. This not only helps the authors, but of course also future readers. Therefore, I would be extremely grateful for a review on this book. Thank you very much.

I wish you all the best, much joy with the axolotls and the best of health!

Legal Notice

Author: Alina Daria Djavidrad

Contact: Wiesenstr. 6, 45964 Gladbeck, Germany

© 2021 Alina Daria Djavidrad

1st edition (2021)